HAPPINESS ,THE BEST CHOICE

A guide for lasting happiness for home ,teens , couple you can count on

JAMES BLESSINGS

TABLE OF CONTENT

.CHAPTER 1

WHY IS IT HARD TO BE HAPPY?

A large portion of us misunderstands bliss. This is because we were raised to believe that life should encourage us. We might have been instructed to keep away from torment at all costs since pessimistic occasions cause gloomy feelings, and gloomy sentiments are not intended to be felt. The outcome might be that we grow up tormented and unwilling and we disintegrate at the earliest hints of pressure because our profound preparation wheels won't ever fall off.

While detours to joy do exist, the uplifting news is they are generally inside our control. Here is a gander at the normal hoodlums of satisfaction and how to change them to feel improved.

1. Dread

It is typical to Fear change. It isn't to Stay buried in wretchedness. Normal purposes behind it incorporate apprehension about the obscure, disappointment, what individuals might express, and of ing a chance with our familiar object for the sake of security and consistency.

Dread handicapped people numerous treatment clients: Staying in a spirit-sucking vocation since "that is how my folks accommodated the family," or staying with despondent connections since "it's better compared to being separated from everyone else," and slowing down on an imaginative endeavor since "what will the cynics say assuming l fizzle?"

It takes fortitude to stride beyond your usual range of familiarity, however, your usual range of familiarity is likewise your risk zone. One of the greatest second thoughts of the withering is remembering all the uncertainties. Besting the rundown is the feeling of dread toward being reprimanded by others. Take a tip from the spouse of an ex-president, Eleanor Roosevelt: "You wouldn't stress such a great amount over others' thought process of you if you understood how rare they do."

2. Pursuing confidence

"It has nearly turned into a cliché in our way of life that we want to have high confidence to be content and sound. However, as the examination is presently beginning to illustrate, the need to constantly assess ourselves emphatically comes at an excessive cost. The principal issue is that having high confidence requires feeling extraordinary or more normal. To be called normal is viewed as an affront to our way of life. This need to feel predominant outcomes in a course of social correlation in which we ceaselessly attempt to puff ourselves up and put others down."

The issue is when our confidence slips, as it definitely will, we begin to incorporate pessimistic sentiments and we are prepared to feel restless, discouraged, and dishonorable.

What's the counteractant?

Foster self-sympathy.

Self-sympathy means to see ourselves as everything being equal, and similarly as questionable as anyone else or a lady. The vibe and great feelings of self-empathy are profoundly steady since they depend on our natural self-esteem.

3. Outside remunerations
Bliss is inside work. Sure a brand new vehicle, smooth digs and a European get-away can improve life, however, they are transitory fixes. Once in a while, we go such a long way beyond our psyches looking for the joy that these outer pursuits block our

way. The best things in life are made and developed — great, strong connections, positive encounters, and adoring recollections. Material merchandise won't give us feel-great feelings and significance.

4. "At the point when I arrive at this objective... "
Life doesn't respect the ideal time. Hanging tight for what's to come in to sit with nervousness, while the world cruises by. We delay our bliss until a period in the future when everything is perfect. Just that opportunity won't ever show up.

Some accept that joy should be acquired, and enduring now implies we can trade out our karmic daylight tomorrow. Satisfaction isn't spiritualist or destined. Restless treatment clients will frequently behave destructively when things begin to turn upward because they accept assuming they underestimate close-to-home wellbeing, the Happiness Gods will strike. Precautionary stressing is an exercise in futility if at any point there was one.

the article goes on after commercial

At a point when I was a youngster, I continually anticipated achievements: secondary school graduation from living, marriage, travel, life as a parent, and so on. Then one day in my 20s I awakened and acknowledged I was living in "the future." And regardless of the achievements, there were consistent obstructions.
When one test was survived, the following was thumping on my front entryway. Also, that acknowledgment constrained me into defective reality, also called the present time and place. Becoming involved with tomorrow's game is so natural. And meanwhile, the present valuable minutes are cruising us by.

5. Negative contemplations

A critical mental example is discovering that our contemplations structure our feelings. It's generally expected to accept that we can't help our sentiments, yet this is just false. Negative considerations can appear to be programmed because they've become imbued in our perspective.

One of the most outstanding ways of combatting persistent negative reasoning is to visit a specialist. A talented specialist will assist you with uncovering your manners of thinking so these considerations can be inspected and managed.

For instance, you might have encountered numerous contemplations after perusing, 'visit a specialist.' Perhaps you had a negative guiding involvement with the past, or your quick idea was, 'oh well, business as usual, somebody letting me know I'm insane, and I want to sort out,' or different considerations which set off a negative affiliation. Assuming that you end up responding to similar individuals and circumstances, again and again, your contemplations are probably hindering your direction.

The nature of our viewpoints means the world to satisfaction.

6. Examination
At any point do you look at Instagram and suppose, "Goodness, if by some stroke of good luck my life was like this and that, then, at that point, I'd truly be blissful"?

We are besieged with updates that our better self is standing ready. Truly, we're seeing altered reality. A valid example: While composing this article I was battling with inspiration. So I headed outside and began taking pictures to post via web-based entertainment. At the point when I checked my mindfulness, I needed to concede I was more worried about arriving at the number of supporters my companions have than with carrying worth to my crowd. Rather than feeling appreciative that I'm ready to compose for cool destinations like the Huffington Post and Psychology Today, I was pursuing more perusers, more likes, more hearts, and more offers. Examination truly is the cheat of satisfaction.

7. Living previously
Not many things are more troubled than seeing somebody trapped in an unending pattern of replaying their great days. As the adage goes, 'youth is squandered on the youthful.' what about the past we would all return and change the unpalatable parts if we would be able. Lamenting what you did or didn't do is pointless because you were an alternate individual in those days. Furthermore, we are continually advancing.

But John from secondary school will cheerfully offer you a brew in return for standing by listening to him discuss that time he made the game-dominating score in the last seconds of the final quarter. Or on the other hand, how his life is undeniably messed up because of that pitiful spouse who turned his children against him and swindled him during the separation.

Try not to be that person.

8. Free limits
Sound limits are the way to bliss. Without a diagram for what our identity is, who we are not, and who and what we need in our life, we basically can't oversee time and close-to-home energy.

For instance, suppose you and your family headed out across town to visit your people for Sunday supper. What's more, after dessert Mom doesn't believe that you should leave, even though your children are grumpy. At the point when Mom pushes limits that adversely influence your family, stay firm, however adoring: "I value the time we had today, yet as I referenced previously, sleep time is at 8:00 p.m. what's more, we need to get moving."

Mother might consider limits to be a test, and encouragement to provoke you. Hold your ground and force "second level" limits, if important. For instance, leave without participating in any further discussion, switch off your cell phone, and don't permit yourself to be coerced into rehashed supplications to make an exemption since "it's an extraordinary event."

9. Disregarding appreciation
There's an entire host of motivations behind why we ought to make appreciation a day-to-day practice — research has shown that being grateful emphatically affects our prosperity.

At the point when we flounder in what we don't have, we waste our profound energies. Zeroing in on our weaknesses as opposed to our favors implies failing to focus on the way that most things in our lives are very great.

Take a stab at considering three things every day that you're thankful for or keep an appreciation journal. These little demonstrations require only minutes, yet the distinction in standpoint and positive feelings can have a major effect.

10. Disregarding the cycle
Once in a while, we make life harder than needed. Joy isn't a necessary evil, for there is no Destination Happy. Sure we experience happy minutes and euphoric recollections, yet life is about the excursion and partaking in the means en route. At the point when we let go of our restricted perspective on joy, we acknowledge that life is brimming with recurring patterns where occasionally are perfect, others are great, and some are terrible. What's more, that is fine. Developing joy is as much about

dealing with affliction as it's worth
embracing excellence in regular minutes.

******

CHAPTER 2

ATTITUDES OF UNHAPPY PEOPLE

1. Foolish Talk

Foolish talk is involved messages we ship off ourselves which lessen our certainty, reduce our presentation, bring down our true capacity, and at last harm our prosperity. Normal pointless talk incorporates sentence starting points, for example,

"I can't... "

"I'm not sufficient... "

"I'm not certain ... "

"I don't have the stuff... "

"I will come up short... "

Could you like it assuming that a companion tells you over and over that "you will fail," "you're not sufficient," "you need certainty," "you don't have the stuff," or "you will fizzle?" Would you think about this individual as a genuine companion? If not, how could you like to talk or think as such to yourself? Participating in routine pointless talk resembles having a bogus companion who puts you during throughout the entire time. You become your most terrible adversary and doubter.

2. Negative Assumptions

An overarching type of negative reasoning is to check out a circumstance or cooperation and assume the negative. For some individuals, this "taking a gander at the glass half vacant" mentality is ongoing and programmed. One could take a gander at a packed drive, a blustery day, or cover the bills as programmed negative encounters.

There's nothing intrinsically sure or negative about traffic, climate, or bill paying. As the adage goes, "what will be will be." It's how you decide to connect with your conditions that makes the experience positive or negative. This decision can immediately make you more grounded or more vulnerable, more joyful or gloomier, engaged or exploited. Given similar circumstances, one could view a jam-packed drive as an opportunity to pay attention to loosening up music or practice careful breathing; a stormy day as an event to twist up at home with hot chocolate and a decent book, or bill paying as a chance to rehearse the "pay yourself first" establishing financial stability technique. It's all by the way you decide to connect with the occasion.

3. Negative Comparison with Others

One of the least demanding and most well-known ways of genuinely regretting oneself is to contrast yourself horribly with others. We might be enticed to contrast ourselves and the people who have more achievements, appear to be more alluring, get more cash flow, or brag more Facebook companions.

At the point when you end up wishing to have what another person has and feel envious, mediocre, or insufficient as the outcome, you're having a pessimistic social examination second.

Research demonstrates that constant pessimistic social correlations can make an individual encounter more prominent pressure, uneasiness, sorrow, and pursue reckless decisions

4. Negative Rumination about the Past

We ought to gain from an earlier time, however not be trapped in it. Here and there life conditions and individual misfortunes can torment and keep us from seeing our actual potential and perceiving new open doors. What has proactively happened we can't change, yet what is yet to happen we can shape and impact. Now and again the initial step is basically to part from an earlier time and pronounces that it is you, not your set of experiences, who's in control. Goethe reminds us: "Nothing is worth more than this day." Don't choose to move on. Settle on better decisions today and continue.

"Abraham Lincoln lost eight races, bombed two times in business, and experienced a mental meltdown before he turned into the leader of the United States."

5. Debilitating Beliefs about Difficult People

The vast majority of us experience troublesome individuals in our lives. Despite such testing people, it's enticing to accept that they are the culprits and we are the people in question, or that they hold the power with their difficult way of behaving. Such mentalities, regardless of whether supported, are receptive and along these lines self-debilitating.

The way to change your debilitating convictions about troublesome individuals is to move from being receptive to proactive. Whether you're managing an egomaniac, an uninvolved forceful, a controller, or a scary and controlling oppressor, there are numerous abilities and procedures you can use to keep steady over the circumstance.

6. The Desire to Blame

Fault can be characterized as considering others answerable for our disasters. Certain individuals cast their useless guardians, negative connections, financial impediments, well-being challenges, or other life difficulties as the justification for their misery and absence of achievement.

While it's positively a fact that life presents numerous hardships, and unquestionable the agony and enduring they frequently cause, to fault others as the justification behind one's despondency is to project oneself in the job of the person in question.

There are deceptive benefits to exploitation, as blame shifting gives advantageous support to life's unacceptable circumstances, and sheds the work important to take total charge of one's own life and prosperity.

Be that as it may, routine accusing after some time sustains sharpness, hatred, and frailty, as the casualty experiences.

Frequently, the individuals who are the objective of your fault have little thought (or could mind less) about how you truly feel. You just hurt yourself by being your very own detainee harshness and hatred. Your sentiments might be legitimate, yet they won't assist you with becoming cheerful, sound, and fruitful. Eventually, isn't that the thing you truly care about?

"At the point when we fault, we offer our power.

7. The Struggle to Forgive Yourself

We all commit errors throughout our everyday life. At the point when you glance back at your past deeds, maybe there were choices and activities you lament. There might have been sad blunders in judgment. You might have hurt yourself as well as others.

As you review these previous occasions, there might be a going with healthy identity fault for the bungles made, the harm done, or open doors missed. You could consider yourself a "terrible" or "defective" individual and flounder in responsibility. During these minutes, it's critical to be humane with yourself, knowing that now that you're more mindful, you get an opportunity to try not to rehash previous oversights and to have a constructive outcome with yourself as well as other people.

8. The Fear of Failure and Making Mistakes

The anxiety toward disappointment and committing errors is frequently connected with compulsiveness (to some extent in specific parts of your life). You might feel that you're not sufficient somehow or another, in this way putting gigantic strain on yourself to succeed.

While setting elevated expectations can act as a powerful inspirational apparatus, anticipating that yourself should be amazing removes the delight from life, and can restrict your most noteworthy potential for progress. Different examinations have shown the relationship among's compulsiveness and despondency. Attempt as we would, it essentially isn't human to be awesome, and positively not constantly.

"Given the longing to be esteemed and appreciated, it's enticing to attempt to seem, by all accounts, to be awesome, yet the expenses of such duplicities are high... How could you at any point such as yourself when you don't come.

CHAPTER 3

KEYS TO HAPPINESS

A great many people need to be content. Be that as it may, they likewise need to find true success. Furthermore, while every individual could have an individualized meaning of exactly how every one of those things affects them explicitly, the general longing to have an existence that is liberated from pressure, stress, nervousness, and dread, while being loaded with satisfaction and achievement, is steady.

In any case, even though we should be blissful and effective throughout everyday life, that is frequently distant from the case. Ordinarily, we invest a greater amount of our energy saturated with pessimistic feelings than we do in the good ones. From our connections to our funds, our professions, our wellbeing, and our objectives, we frequently apparently can't beat the pressure related to regular worries.

Couple all of that with our expectations and our fantasies for the future, and the steady disappointments that we face en route while attempting to accomplish anything prominent, and it's no big surprise we invest quite a bit of our energy despondent and feeling ineffective. So how would we approach doing the inverse? What are the keys to joy and achievement? What's more, is that something achievable throughout everyday life?

There are 7 fundamental keys to bliss and achievement that will assist with emerging both those things in your day-to-day existence.

1 — Gratitude
Satisfaction and achievement are gone before appreciation. We want to cheerfully succeed instead of attempting to prevail to be content. Achievement shouldn't raise bliss. Bliss ought to bread achievement.

When we're cheerful, and we're accomplishing something we love throughout everyday life, achievement turns into a side-effect. Nonetheless, when our bliss relies on our prosperity, beneficial things won't ever come.

It's likewise an issue of concentration. What have we centered around throughout everyday life? What do we need the most? Also, what are the explanations behind zeroing in on and needing those things? At the point when we center around what we don't have, we live in that frame of mind of need. We understand exactly the amount we're passing up or the amount we miss the mark on assets to do the things that we truly care about.

2 — Be Present

There's not at all like becoming involved with the past or continually agonizing over the future that more than ruins the current second. However at that point once more, large numbers of us have inconvenience basic being available. We can't see the value in the present time and place. Normally, we're more stressed over what will happen tomorrow or what happened yesterday instead of halting and being available.

However, what's the significance here to be available? What's more, for what reason is this one of the keys to joy and achievement? All things considered, like the basic demonstration of appreciation, being available grounds us at the time. We stop to see the value in the supernatural occurrences that exist toward each path we look at, the excellence of the relative multitude of things around us, and the excursion that we call life. It assists us with rising above the apprehensions of tomorrow and the second thoughts of yesterday.

3 – Manage Time Effectively
One propensity that will impact both your satisfaction and your general outcome

throughout everyday life, is the capacity to successfully oversee time. Successful time chiefs have an idea about their commitments throughout everyday life and know exactly how to shuffle things to excel. They center around their drawn-out objectives and focus on the exercises that will assist with pushing them ahead as opposed to abandoning them.

At the point when we don't deal with our time, we improve our probability of stress, tension, dread, and stress. We get so up to speed in the everyday demonstration of answering life's stressors, that we can't prudently handle the things that will assist with staying away from emergencies and crises from here on out. We miss bill installments, disregard gatherings, and neglect to coordinate our exercises to seek after our drawn-out objectives.

4 – Set SMARTER Goals

Frequently, what keeps us away from making progress throughout everyday life, is anything we could characterize that is similar to, our failure to define objectives the correct way. In a new report, it was resolved that just 8% of individuals who put forth objectives on New Year's Eve accomplish them. However, past those New Year's objectives, we as a whole realize that many individuals frequently put forth objectives yet don't accomplish them.

Certainly, you've laid out an objective before and you abandoned it. We all have. Yet, it's the objective-setting process that disrupted the general flow. At the point when we put forth detached objectives, in that we don't lay out the objectives on paper and don't characterize the energetically, nor make an arrangement for their fulfillment, we will quite often either fall flat or abandon them. Be that as it may, for individuals who put forth objectives the correct way, the

SMARTER way, the achievement is undeniably more feasible.

5 — Embody an Empowering Morning Routine

Everything starts and finishes with an enabling morning schedule. What you do toward the beginning of the day, establishes the rhythm until the end of the day. Thus, it directs the result of your life. To be content and effective, make a bunch of propensities in the first part of the day to assist with cultivating that in your life. The right mix of propensities executed every day of the week can have a significant effect.

We're such predictable animals, that we neglect to do the things that will benefit our lives since we get up to speed doing the things that we're so used to. We're saturated with propensity and schedule, and not ones that serve us. Generally, we're too occupied with answering life and its mind-boggling requests on us, to take the bulls by the horn, as it were.

6 — Tackle the Most important task of the day

otherwise called the main undertakings of the day, is a vital piece of achievement. They offer one of the most urgent keys to accomplishing our objectives in life over the long haul. It's not generally simple to pursue the MITs, particularly when we feel so worried or overpowered by life. Be that as it may, it's a fundamental demonstration assuming that we will get where we want to go.

7 — Focus on Health and Wellbeing

Well-being and prosperity are significant pieces of the joy and-achievement equation, and one of the greatest keys to accomplishing them both. At the point when we cause things to damage ourselves by gorging, over-drinking liquor, consuming sporting medications, and so forth, in addition to the fact that it antagonistically affects our bodies, yet in addition on our psyches.

CHAPETR 4

MAKING LIFE MORE MEANINGFUL

The most effective method to make life significant

We as a whole need to carry on with a significant life, yet a great many people don't sort out some way to go about it.

What is a significant life
Each individual has an alternate comprehension of life, contingent upon

their point of view. In any case, there's agreement on what a significant life is.

Life has meaning when it is huge, makes an effect, and has an effect — on you and others.

Everybody alive is carrying on with life, yet not every person feels satisfied. Furthermore, the explanation is easy to perceive.

Running vast patterns of work-eat-rest rehash doesn't deliver your life meaning however it keeps you occupied.

Simply floating through existence with no heading or reason will prompt discontent and despondency.

You want a higher reason to seek after to encounter a feeling of satisfaction. An inclination that you are utilizing your life, delivering your gifts and capacities, and utilizing them successfully to have a scratch and an effect, will give pleasure to your reality.

The following are 6 different ways you can make your life more significant.

1. Quit living on autopilot mode
"If you are not deliberately coordinating your life, you will lose your balance, and conditions will choose for you."

Carrying on with life that goes here and there aimlessly and runs precisely has no intrinsic importance. You feel unchallenged and deadened carrying on with such a tasteless life.

To make your life more significant, switch off the autopilot mode and carry on with life proactively by being available in your life and pursuing cognizant decisions.

Develop a development mentality, get out of your usual range of familiarity and investigate fresher open doors and conceivable outcomes. This will assist you with pushing your limits and empower you to succeed at what you do.

You have endless potential locked inside you; stretch your cutoff points and draw out the best in you.

Putting resources into self-development isn't just a significantly fulfilling experience, however, it likewise assists you with getting on to a higher degree of progress and bliss.

3. Seek after things that matter
It's not difficult to lose all sense of direction in the labyrinth of life when there's no clearness about what you need throughout everyday life.

Running behind the thing everybody is frantically chasing after leads you on a way that wastes your time. It will just prompt misery and dissatisfaction.

To give importance to your life, center around things that hold importance for yourself and can assist with bettering your life.

Life becomes satisfying when you remain nearby your qualities and desires and expect to arrive at objectives that you truly put stock in. This will put forth the attempts productive and the existing venture beneficial.

3. Quit thinking, begin living
Many individuals carry on with a disappointed life since they overthink and excessively center around what's on the horizon for them or how things would end up.

To carry on with a significant life, you should relinquish the fanciful feelings of trepidation and concerns and set out on the excursion to progress.

Issues and challenges will undoubtedly come in your direction when you step out into the unexplored world. Shrewdness lies in exploring the difficulties and tracking down your strategy for getting around the deterrents.

The way to our objective isn't a straight one all of the time. We go down some unacceptable street; we get lost, and we turn around. Perhaps it doesn't make any difference which street we leave on. Perhaps what makes a difference is that we leave."

4. Increase the value of others
Everyone can help other people and be of worth to them. Everything necessary is a shift of concentration from your needs, needs, wants, and thinking magnanimously, to loan some assistance to other people.

At the point when you are purposeful about helping other people, there's no restriction to what you can do.

It doesn't be guaranteed to must be monetary assistance; you can enhance others in numerous alternate ways. The charitable effort, show somebody significant expertise, guide them by your experience ice, and sand hare your errors and illustrations learned.

In the case of nothing else, elevate others' spirits, give trust, and rouse them to seek after their objectives.

It's your method for communicating your human side and letting others in on you give it a second thought.

The substance of carrying on with a significant life is realizing that you and your work matter and that you can affect the existence of people around you.

5. Make never-ending bonds
We are in general friendly creatures; in this way, creating significant associations is critical in carrying on with significant life.

Holding with friends and family and similar individuals provides you with a feeling of having a place and sharing your considerations, thoughts, sentiments, and feelings with them, subsequently giving a satisfying encounter.

Living in a close relationship with your family and individuals from your care group gives profound security and lifts your bliss as you are most likely awesome some individuals care are who have you covered.

6. Weave your satisfaction
An excessive number of individuals trust that excessively lengthy for others will fulfill them. All they end up with is disillusionment and misery.

To make a significant life, take the responsibility for life in your grasp and acknowledge full liability regarding what occurs in your life.

At the point when you comprehend that your joy depends on you and it comes from the inside, you'll quit looking for it beyond you. This will radically lessen your reliance on others, and they'll start to let completely go over you.

Try not to allow anybody to come in the method of your carrying on with a full life. Make your bliss by participating in significant pursuits and accomplishing the work that you view as satisfying.

Work and life are beneficial when there is an association between the two s and one upholds the other.

"Very little is expected to make a blissful life; it is all inside yourself."

Shutting TAUGHT
Life is significant when it sounds valid to you and causes you to feel satisfied. Genuine bliss lies in making the best of what life offers you.

The excursion of life is all that is significant and it becomes advantageous when you can enjoy the excursion, think back, and tell yourself you gave your all.

In this manner, zeroing in on the right things and having made something critical of your life — without feeling any lament — best epitomizes a significant life."Life is like a camera. Focus on what's important. Capture the good times. And if things don't work out, take another shot."

www.ingramcontent.com/pod-product-compliance
Lightning Source LLC
LaVergne TN
LVHW052107160826
845678LV00015B/3404

* 9 7 9 8 3 5 1 6 2 0 0 6 0 *